There Goes A Mermaid!

~ A NorFolktale ~

by Lisa Suhay

Illustrations by
Sam Hundley

First Edition

Published by The Virginian-Pilot

Library of Congress Control Number: 2004108840

Author: Lisa Suhay
Book Design: Kira Porter
Book Production: Peri Poloni, Knockout Design, www.knockoutbooks.com

Printed in Singapore

To Bess and Peter Decker - for believing in mermaids and introducing them to the City of Norfolk, Virginia.
For the artists, dreamers and mermaid nurturers who have kept the magic alive and well.

Zoltan, Ian, Avery and Quin from Mommy. Robert, thanks, you were right.
A hug to Margaret Pidgeon for making us feel at home.
- Lisa Suhay

NOTE TO READERS:
A book so nice you can read it twice!
The main story surrounds the mermaids.

A poem flows in the water on every page.

KEVIN GALLUP created the basic sculpture form for all the Norfolk Mermaids.
There are now over 300 mermaid sculptures in and around the City of Norfolk, Virginia and counting.

The artists and the original titles for the mermaids in this book are listed below.

JOHN HICKEY – Maid of Brass
(from which the cover illustration was drawn)

KEN WRIGHT – Flying Spirit (Title page)

SHARON FRANKLIN – Spoken Word
(Dedication page)

SHERRY HODGES – Sea Shimmer (p 1)

MICHELE BARNES – Siren (p 2)

DAVE IWANS – Yuma Ya (p 3)

JENNIFER BLYTHE – Of the Sea (p 4)

CYNTHIA GRAF – Ocean Patina (p 7)

BESS DECKER – Princess Azalea (p 8)

RYAN BRINKLEY – Mirror Mosaic (p 9)

TERRY COX–JOSEPH – Catch of the Day (p 10)

JOSCELYN L. RIVERS – Tiger Wood (p 10)

BEN TEAGUE – Candybar (p 11)

TERRY COX–JOSEPH – Fish Dish (p 12)

KIMBERLY KANE – By the Stars (p 13)

ED BEARDSLEY – Penny (p 14)

KOREEN D'AMILLIO – Hats Off to the Navy (p 15)

MYKE IRVING – Flower Garden (p 16)

AMY TARDY – Seasonal Maid (p 16)

DEBORAH T. SMALL – Literacy (p 17)

CYNTHIA GRAF – Jewel of the Sea (p 18)

PAMELA PINE WINSLOW – Liquid Energy
(p 29 after the tips where it says Good Luck!)

STEVEN F. MORRIS – A New Horizon
(Downtown map page)

All around the city, mermaid sculptures stretch out their arms, long hair waving, tails held high as if swimming in the sky.

Tails. Scales. Long wavy hair.

People pass them every day and cry, "There goes a mermaid!"
They don't know how right they are.

Mermaids! Mermaids! Everywhere!

These statues are more than just artworks. They are really mermaids' city apartments.

The pipes holding them in place go to the river and on to the sea.

Art apartments in the city: shiny, scaly, glittery, pretty.

Only artists will do for creating their homes. Norfolk has lots of artists.
Here's how it's done. Mermaids are shape-changers.
Some old stories call them Selchies (SELL-KEYS) and tell of them turning into seals.

Our city mermaids do
much more than that!

Ocean's daughters turn to water and through the pipes they swim.

The mermaid only has to touch dry land to make her tail instantly transform into legs and her shells and beads change to stylish clothes.

Land ho! Scales and tails go. Maids turn to women. No more swimmin'!

The mermaid picks an artist, pays in sea treasure and slips back into the harbor.

There, she waits for the artist to finish her apartment and drop a key with her name on it into the water.

They use treasure to buy their keys.

The mermaid unlocks her pipe. She turns into water and flows through the pipes and up into her apartment.

So the next time you pass a Norfolk mermaid, put your ear to her and see if you can hear the ocean.

Listen to a mermaid. Hear the seas?

How does she get out and why don't we see her appear? Excellent questions!

Check the statues for tearstains.
The mermaids cry themselves out
of the statue's eyes - drip, drip, drip.

They touch the ground
and materialize in a blink.

Can you spot the ocean's daughter?

Some mermaids had their artist add hundreds of tiny mirrors and shiny bits to their sculpture so that the sun would dazzle your eyes at just the right moment and make you miss their appearance.

With all that magic, sunlight and mirrors, even the most observant person could miss the trick!

Eyes like sun on the water.

An important fact to know when mermaid spotting:
Each mermaid's house is not an exact portrait of herself (though some are).
Most are fashioned after what the mermaid does for a living. City mermaids have jobs.

Some work at the zoo,
because fur and feathers are
fascinating to sea dwellers.

Their homes match what they do. These two work at the zoo.

And since you can't get chocolate under water,
mermaids often choose to work in candy shops.

Marina makes candies that are new.

Baking in the sea is also rather difficult,
so Rowena the mermaid moved to
Ghent to make cakes day and night.

Rowena serves afternoon tea.

Because they are such good friends with artists,
they often work at museums.

Kira has art you must see!

Bank mermaids are happiest when children come in
to get change to toss into fountains,

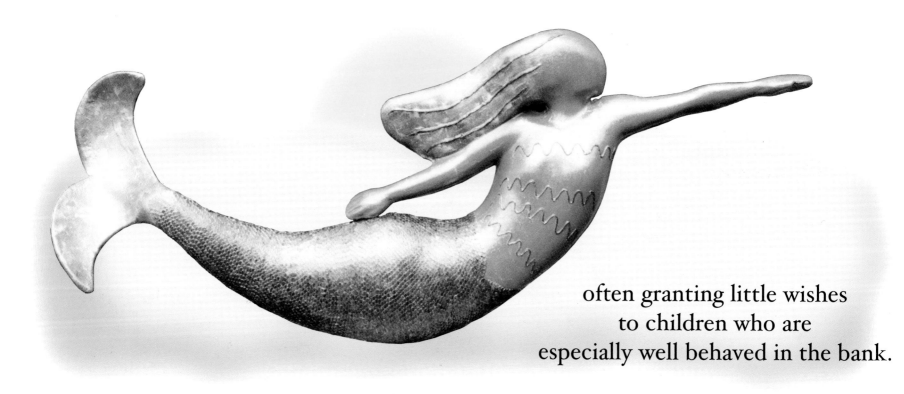

often granting little wishes
to children who are
especially well behaved in the bank.

Working at the bank, there's Penny. She grants wishes, but not too many.

There are mermaids in the Navy.
Some guard the harbor.

Others go with the ships
on missions out to sea, keeping
them safe in stormy times.

Oceana protects ships with her powers.

Have you seen the flower mermaids who tend the Botanical Garden?
Can you guess which apartments are theirs?

Others love to tend the flowers.

Surely you've seen the ones teaching in our
schools and working in the public libraries.

No? Well, maybe
you just need some
more tips for
recognizing them.

Teaching. Reading. Everywhere!

Once you know their secrets, maybe you can catch a mermaid appearing.
If you do, she may grant you a wish.

If she asks how
you learned her secrets,
tell her you read it
in a fish story.

They picked our city 'cause they know we care.

 # Mermaid Spotter's Guide

Tip #1

Mermaids are all ages, colors and sizes.
Some of the mermaids living inside the sculptures
are great-great grandmothers!

Tip #2
They are happy. Celebrating life every day, just like they were waking up to a party that never ends.

Tip #3
Their eyes – whether green as the ocean, blue as the sky, grey as a storm cloud or brown as the rocky shore – always have the sparkle of sun on the water. When you look into them, you feel as if you are looking far out to sea.

Tip #4
Their speaking voices are soft as sea foam, but their laughs are wild and free. They sound just like seagulls!

Tip #5
Mermaids listen to the wind, which they call Mermaid's Breath, the way we listen to our favorite music. Ask a mermaid the name of her favorite singer; she will tell you it's "Varuna," a merman from India whose breath blows ships across the ocean. But that is another story!

Tip #6
When a mermaid stands near a fish tank,
all the creatures inside come to her.

Tip #7
Cats love mermaids!
Cats follow them all around and rub against their
legs just as if they were walking cans of tuna.

Tip #8

Because their eyes are used to looking through water, they see better in the rain and often don't use windshield wipers on their cars!

Tip #9

They love salty foods. Mermaids devour whole bags of chips and never get thirsty afterwards!

And finally, Tip #10

When mailing letters or packages,
they spell the name of the town wrong
as a code to their friends.

Instead of Norfolk, Virginia, they write "Merfolk, Virginia."

One story ends and another begins. Time to start your quest for the elusive Norfolk Mermaids. As you drive around Norfolk, mark mermaid homes on the maps.

Good luck!

Remember, mermaids love to change like the wind and tide. Their city apartments shift from place to place like sand on the beach and new ones appear all the time.

Downtown Norfolk ~ Mermaid Spotting Map

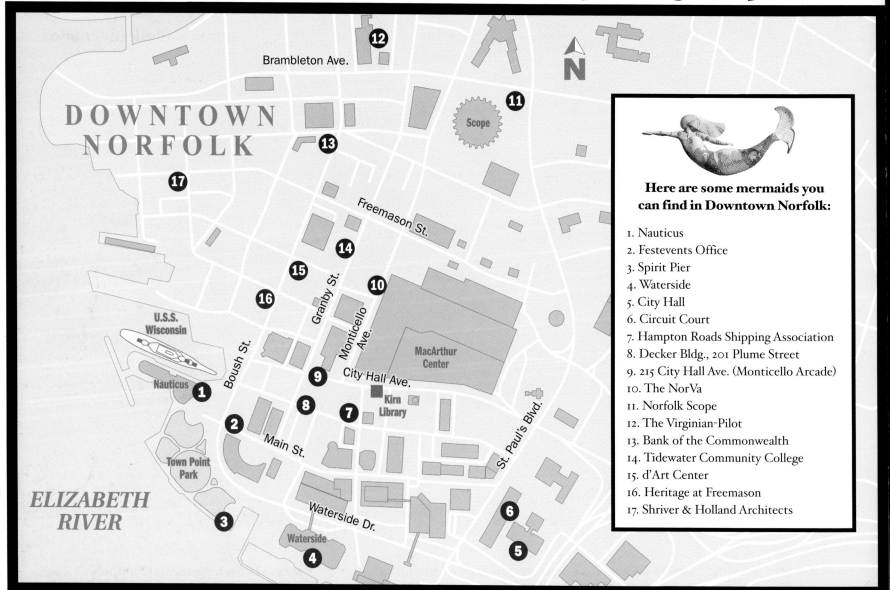

Brambleton Ave.

DOWNTOWN NORFOLK

Scope

Freemason St.

U.S.S. Wisconsin

Nauticus

Boush St.

Granby St.

Monticello Ave.

City Hall Ave.

MacArthur Center

Kirn Library

Main St.

Town Point Park

ELIZABETH RIVER

Waterside Dr.

Waterside

St. Paul's Blvd.

N

Here are some mermaids you can find in Downtown Norfolk:

1. Nauticus
2. Festevents Office
3. Spirit Pier
4. Waterside
5. City Hall
6. Circuit Court
7. Hampton Roads Shipping Association
8. Decker Bldg., 201 Plume Street
9. 215 City Hall Ave. (Monticello Arcade)
10. The NorVa
11. Norfolk Scope
12. The Virginian-Pilot
13. Bank of the Commonwealth
14. Tidewater Community College
15. d'Art Center
16. Heritage at Freemason
17. Shriver & Holland Architects

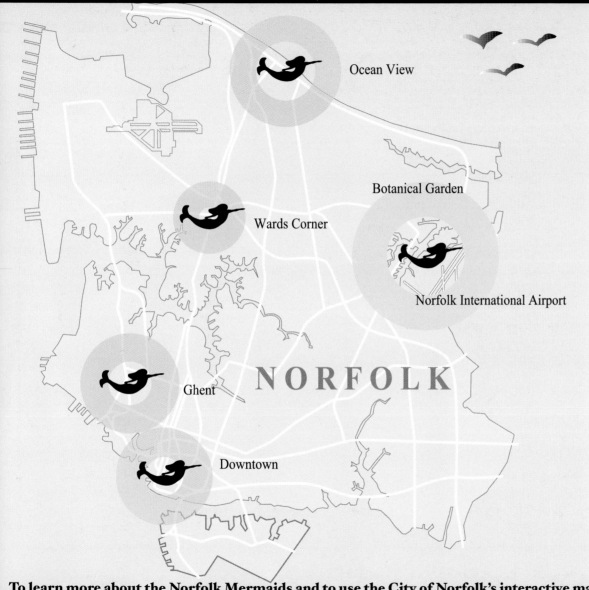

Ocean View

Botanical Garden

Wards Corner

Norfolk International Airport

Ghent

NORFOLK

Downtown

Here are some areas where Norfolk mermaids are likely to be found.

See how many you can spot and then write them down!

_____
_____
_____
_____
_____
_____
_____
_____
_____
_____
_____
_____
_____
_____
_____
_____
_____
_____

To learn more about the Norfolk Mermaids and to use the City of Norfolk's interactive map, visit www.mermaidsonparade.com.

Buying this book helps others through:

The Virginian-Pilot Joy Fund

The Virginian-Pilot Joy Fund has been bringing holiday happiness and gifts to more than one million underprivileged children in Norfolk, Chesapeake, Portsmouth, Suffolk, Virginia Beach, Virginia's Eastern Shore, Isle of Wight County and the City of Franklin since 1934.

You can make your contribution by mailing your check (payable to the Joy Fund) to: the Joy Fund, P.O. Box 2136, Norfolk, Virginia 23501 or go online at PilotOnline.com/joyfund.

&

The Literacy Partnership

The Literacy Partnership's mission is to increase the awareness of literacy programming; promote the benefits of supporting literacy rate improvement to the Hampton Roads regional economy; and enhance the capacity and performance of literacy resources. The Partnership works with RIF (Reading is Fundamental) and is a partner with the Hampton Roads Chamber of Commerce to support Literacy in the Workplace programming. Learn more online at www.theliteracypartnership.org.

Author's Acknowledgements

The author would like to thank those at The Virginian-Pilot who donated their time and talents to create this book/fundraiser. Dee Carpenter, the vision. Pam Smith-Rodden, the courage. Nancy Tatterson and Beverly Shepard, the details. Kira Porter, the design and Sam Hundley, the illustrations. John Earle, the maps. Jeff White, Leo Kim, Chris Henniker and the photography department of The Virginian-Pilot, the mermaid photos. Dan Reeves and Johnny Messina, the color scans. Theirs is a legacy of joy and magic.

Special thanks to Beth Fraim who calmed the waters for this book, and Michelle Carrera, who has been the compass for the author throughout the project. - Lisa Suhay